CREATING A HEALTHY LIFE

The Art and Wisdom of

HOWARD MURAD, M.D.

Wisdom Waters Press, LLC
4712 Admiralty Way, #814
Marina del Rey, CA 90292

Quantity sales. Special discounts are available on quantity purchases by corporations,
associations, and others. For details, contact the "Special Sales Department"
at the address above.

Printed in the United States of America

ISBN: 978-193964-209-7

First Edition

17 16 15 14 13   10 9 8 7 6 5 4 3 2 1

For Loralee

ACKNOWLEDGMENTS

Books, paintings, and ideas are highly personal creations, but they never arise from a vacuum. The writer, artist, or thinker always owes a debt of gratitude to others, and in this case, there are many who have helped along the way. My greatest inspiration has been my beloved wife, Loralee, and I thank her constantly for that and for all she means to me. I thank my father, mother, and family for having taught me the importance of self-reliance and to find beauty and meaning in each day and every circumstance. I also thank my children and grandchildren for reminding me of the endurance and power of youth. I'd like to thank my personal assistant, Kelly Armstrong, and all my coworkers at Murad, Inc., for their friendship, loyalty, and hard work. My sincere thanks to Roy Walkenhorst, Judy Brooks, and Ray Jones for guiding me through the intricate process of writing, assembling, and publishing this book. And finally, I must acknowledge my debt to the thousands of patients I've worked with over the years. They have led me to countless marvelous discoveries, a deeper understanding of medicine, and a fuller appreciation of life and all it represents.

INTRODUCTION

"Living is an art," says Dr. Howard Murad, who treats each day as if it were a canvas to be filled with vibrant colors. He loves life and loves his work, and not surprisingly, he is a very active man. This has always been the case, just as his attitude toward his work and life has always been a positive one.

A prominent Los Angeles physician, Dr. Murad has successfully treated more than 50,000 patients. Drawing on his training as both a pharmacist and physician, he has developed a popular and highly effective line of skincare products that has won praise from health and beauty conscious consumers. A practitioner not just of medicine but of the philosophy of health, Dr. Murad has written four books and hundreds of articles, and earned a worldwide reputation as an authority on slowing the aging process.

Dr. Murad's unique approach to medicine involves a concept he calls Inclusive Health. An alternative to traditional medical practice with its emphasis on the "spot treatment" of individual conditions or illnesses, the Inclusive Health approach treats the whole patient. Among other things, it takes into consideration the patient's diet, lifestyle, and emotional state as well as intracellular water—the hydration level of cells.

Years of painstaking research and experience with thousands of patients have convinced Dr. Murad that human health and happiness are directly linked to the ability of cells to retain water. A poor diet and the stress of day-to-day living can damage the all-important membranes that form cell walls. Over time, the membranes become broken and porous, causing the cells to leak water and lose vitality. This, in turn, leads to accelerated aging and a wide variety of diseases and syndromes.

In his bestseller The Water Secret, published in 2010, Dr. Murad explained how to stop this process—and how to reverse it. It was here that he first focused public attention on Inclusive Health. This groundbreaking concept has three essential components: external, internal, and emotional. The first component involves good skincare practices; the second, a healthy diet emphasizing raw fruits and vegetables; and the third, an overall reduction in stress combined with a more youthful and creative outlook on life.

Given the breakneck pace of modern life, the emotional component is often the most difficult part of the Inclusive Health treatment process to adopt. Our addiction to freeways, computers, cell phones, and fast-paced living places on us an enormous amount of what Dr. Murad describes as cultural stress. To deal with this cultural stress, we live increasingly structured lives that are less and less open to the free play and creativity that make life worth living. We can choose not to live this way. But reducing stress and embracing a more youthful outlook often involves major shifts in lifestyle— changes in jobs, accommodations, locales, hobbies, habits, and relationships. It may even require a complete personal transformation of the sort sometimes identified with a single galvanizing experience.

A few years ago Dr. Murad himself had just such a transformative experience, one that began in the unlikeliest of ways. In the following narrative, he tells the story of that experience and how it refocused his thinking and brought years of medical inquiry and research into clearest focus. In his own words, he explains how everyone can live healthier, happier, and more vigorous lives through Inclusive Health and a process he calls Youth Building.

A Change in Perspective

Life is art.

Life may not be a painting, a sculpture, a novel, or a piece of music, but it has a lot in common with these things because living is a creative undertaking. Each new day presents us with a blank canvas, and it is up to us to fill it with shapes, colors, work, play, and joy.

External forces and events beyond our control also influence our days and sometimes bring hardship and sorrow. Even so, we remain

the artists. In the end, how we live and how we respond to the challenges of life is up to us.

I didn't always know this about life. After all, life is not only a creative enterprise—it's also a learning process. Throughout my life, I've tried to keep learning, and over the years I've found that many of the really important things I've discovered haven't come from books or lectures but from my own personal experiences.

Several years ago, I had an experience that profoundly changed the way I look at life, interact with others, and approach the practice of medicine. It helped me see everything more clearly and tap a hidden personal potential that I had hardly known existed.

During the fall of 2008 I began to have serious trouble with my eyes. I was on a trip to Hong Kong when I noticed that my vision had suddenly gotten blurry. So I called my wife, Loralee, and asked her to make me an appointment with an eye doctor.

The diagnosis was a detached retina, which required immediate surgery to save my eyesight. After the operation, I was forced to keep my head down with my chin on my chest for nearly a month while the retina healed. This was painful and, of course, it forced me to sharply limit my activities. But I had to do it. It was either that or risk losing the vision in the affected eye altogether.

An experience like that would be difficult for anyone, but it was especially hard on me. I've always been a very energetic and active man, so the lack of mobility—not being able to work, exercise, and follow my usual routine—was, to say the least, challenging. Somehow I had to find an interesting way to fill the hours. Loralee suggested I use some of the time for art.

A year or so earlier we had taken an art lesson at a spa in Ojai, California. I had never thought of myself as the art type or as someone whose creative instincts leaned in that direction, but we took the class. It was a very basic lesson and lasted only about an hour. The teacher introduced us to a few materials and techniques and then left us on our own.

At the end of the hour I had completed eleven pieces. My teacher, Renate Collins, glanced at them and said, "I don't recommend you take any formal art classes because they will spoil you. Your style is unique and lessons will ruin it."

Dr. Murad completed this piece and the artwork shown on pages 3 and 5 during a one-hour art class in Ojai, California, in 2006. Afterwards his teacher told him not to take any more classes because it might ruin his natural style.

She said the best way for me to learn art was by doing it. That way my style would be entirely my own, rather than something I'd acquired from somebody else. She offered a few suggestions on what sort of paper and equipment to buy, but that was about it.

When I got home, I bought some paints, paper, and other art materials but put them all aside and didn't pick them up again for more than a year. Then came the retinal detachment, the surgery, and the long hours of inactivity with little or nothing to do to pass the time. At first I resisted the idea, but finally I decided that Loralee was right—I should use this opportunity to try my hand at art.

As it happened, I enjoyed the art so much that once I got started I couldn't stop. I didn't want to stop because I had found a delightful new way to bring play back into my life. I had discovered something totally unexpected about myself, and my life journey had taken an exciting new turn.

"My Left Leg Still Works"

Over the years my personal journey has taken quite a few turns. The journey began in Iraq, where I was born in 1939. My family had lived there for many generations, but at that time the Middle East was changing even more rapidly than it is today. In 1946, when I was seven years old, we immigrated—fortunately to the United States. It was either leave when we did or never have a chance to leave. It was basically a matter of survival.

We came from relative wealth, and in Iraq we had a nice home and servants. My father was in the import/export business, and he did well, but all that changed quickly after we left Iraq. Within a year, my father was completely broke. At first we lived in a large house on Long Island with a big porch and lots of windows, but we had to move out because of my father's financial difficulties. We ended up living in a 600-square-foot apartment in the New York City borough of Queens.

We were a family of eight: a husband, wife, and six children—I was the youngest of the six—crammed into a tiny apartment on an upper floor of a building with an elevator that never worked.

My father delivered messages in Manhattan for 75 cents an hour, which was then the minimum wage. Of course, there was no fax or email in those days, and he performed more or less the same function, carrying messages—often hurriedly scribbled onto a piece of paper—from one office to another in different parts of the city. That was a long fall for someone who had previously been a successful businessman, but my father was always a happy person, and despite his reversal of fortune, he never lost that quality.

Many years ago, I wrote a story about my father that appeared in *Reader's Digest*. It was a true story about the day my father was mugged in the subway on the way home from work. He was in his seventies at the time. Somebody took his money—he must have had a few dollars with him that day—beat him up, chipped his teeth, and broke his glasses. He barely managed to drag himself home and up the steps to our little apartment. My mother and the rest of us were frantic, because he really was in terrible shape. Even so, what he said to us was this: "Don't worry about it; my left leg still works."

No matter how desperate the situation, my father never failed to look at the positive side of things. I feel fortunate that he passed that attitude along to the rest of us. It helped me to see opportunity where others saw obstacles. It helped me to push past failures and not let them block the road to success.

In school I was a good student, but all along I worked to earn a little spending money and chip in to help the family. For as little as ten cents an hour, I worked as a newspaper delivery boy, a pinsetter in bowling alleys, a soda jerk, a golf caddy, a gardener—even as a Fuller Brush salesman in a very poor and dangerous New York

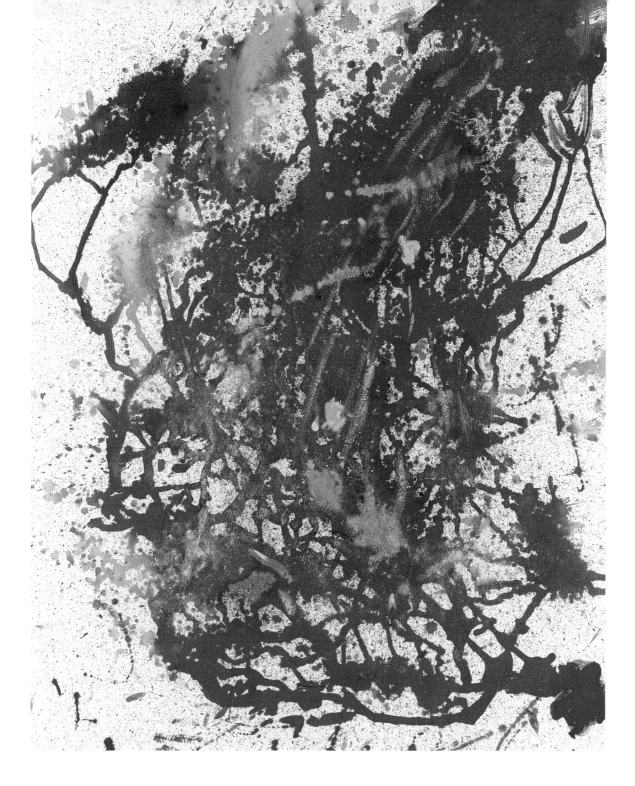

neighborhood. I sometimes worked from eight in the morning until midnight and had to fit my studies in as best I could. I kept working right on through college, pharmacy school, and medical school because I had to pay my own way. But I was sure that all that effort would prove worthwhile. There were opportunities out there, and I wanted to take advantage of them.

When I started college, I thought I wanted to be an engineer. In those days there was a heavy emphasis on engineering because of the space race. The Russians had gotten into space first with Sputnik, and that was seen as a big challenge to America. But because I wasn't able to fully grasp some of the math and physics you need for engineering, that really wasn't the right field for me. As an alternative, my brother Henry mentioned pharmacy school—he was a pharmacist himself—and pointed out that at least I'd have a job when I'd finished. It proved to have been a good suggestion, since I did well in pharmacy school and enjoyed the work. As it turned out, my failure as an engineer wasn't a failure at all because it led to success as a pharmacist. It also started me down the path into medicine.

Even while I was in pharmacy school, I had it in the back of my mind that I wanted to be a doctor. One of my pharmacy school classmates had an uncle who was a successful physician in Los Angeles, and he suggested I apply to medical school. I took his advice, got accepted, and found my life headed in an exciting new direction. As it turned out, medicine had been the right career choice for me all along.

I completed medical school and my internship just about the time the Vietnam War was really heating up. I was given a choice: I could be drafted into the Army as a private or volunteer and serve as a doctor with the rank of Captain. Naturally enough, I volunteered for medical service.

I spent two years in the U.S. Army and a stretch in Vietnam from 1967 to 1968. Right in the middle of that time, the North Vietnamese launched the Tet Offensive, which, of course, was the beginning of the end for the American war effort there. I did my part by serving as a medical officer in the field, performing triage on wounded soldiers, giving them whatever help I could, and passing them along to the Mobile Army Surgical Hospital (MASH). I saw a great deal of suffering out there—far too much.

Vietnam had a big influence on me, in part because I had joined the army as a hawk. Like so many other Americans at that time, it seemed to me we simply had to stop the Communists. I saw plenty of combat and received a Bronze Star for merit and heroism. I was very proud of that at the time and remain proud of it to this day.

I don't remember exactly when my feelings about the war began to change, but I remember all too clearly the day it became obvious to me that they *had* changed.

It was at Phan Thiet in the southeastern part of the country where there was a big American military base and airfield. A young officer came to me with some sort of minor complaint—a cold, I believe. While I was examining him, he told me that he had very recently gotten married, that he was going home soon, and that he was very much looking forward to the life he would live after he got out of the Army. I treated him and he left, but two hours later they brought him back again in a Jeep. He had a very severe wound, and it was immediately obvious to me that, if he survived at all, he would be permanently paralyzed from the neck down.

I had gone into the Army wanting to become a surgeon. But by the time I got back from Vietnam, I'd changed my mind—about the war and about what I wanted to do with my life. All the injuries, blood, and killing had shown me what war was all about, and that, in turn, helped me understand what life was all about. People should have big dreams, but they have to be flexible. My big dream had been to become a physician, but that didn't mean I had to be a surgeon.

Back in the United States where I was stationed at Fort Lewis, Washington, I gave up on the idea of becoming a surgeon as I became increasingly interested in dermatology. Here was a field that would allow me to help people live healthier, happier lives, look better, and feel better about themselves.

Skincare Pioneer

In 1972, following my residency at the UCLA Veterans Administration Hospital, I settled in Los Angeles and opened a dermatology practice. My first office was just 400 square feet and didn't even have a sign on the door. But, over the years, that first small trickle of patients would grow to a steady stream—more than 50,000 patients over four decades.

As my practice grew, I began to take a more expansive view of dermatology and of medicine in general. I could see that the diet, lifestyle, and emotional state of patients had a tremendous impact on their skin and on their overall health. It became obvious that I had to push beyond traditional dermatology with its emphasis on the treatment of individual skin conditions and take the whole patient into consideration. By the 1980s, I had set up what would now be considered a medi spa with an esthetician and electrologist working at my side. Eventually, I opened a full-size independent medical spa that could provide a wide range of treatments and healing experiences.

From the beginning, I had applied my early training as a pharmacist to improve the care my patients received. In many cases, over-the-counter or prescription treatments were either insufficient or completely useless. So I prescribed special compounded treatments that were otherwise unavailable in any form.

During the late 1980s, I created and began to market my own line of skincare products. Many supposedly knowledgeable people, including other physicians, advised me not to do this. They said it couldn't be done or that I couldn't do it. But I had overcome a lot of major obstacles in my life, and ignoring this negative advice, I persevered.

The experience I had with this venture illustrates the point that failure can lead to success. At first I lost money on the business because I didn't know enough about marketing and, frankly, I wasn't a business person. I had to borrow money and refinance my home. It looked as if the whole thing would be a huge failure.

I had tried an infomercial that was very expensive but didn't earn a dime. At this point I thought it might be time to give up on the skin-care products. But I didn't. I was willing to make one more attempt and decided to launch a second infomercial. This one was a hit, and it turned everything around.

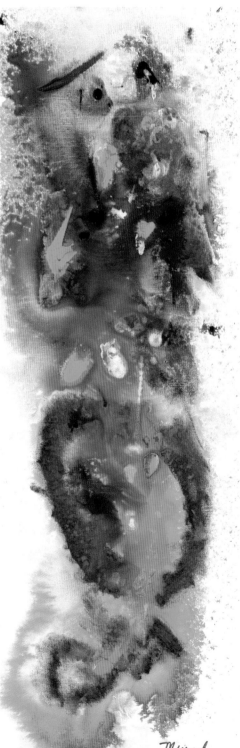

If I had been afraid to try, if I had been afraid of what others were thinking, about what other doctors thought of what I was doing, this could never have happened.

You can't succeed if you're too afraid of failure to take a risk or if you're afraid of what people will think. You have to be comfortable with yourself and with what you are doing rather than just follow the lead of others. To this day people point to the competition and say "they're doing X, Y, and Z." Most brands would follow these trends, but not mine. I create my own trends.

Back then, the salons were mostly focused on moisturizers. When I went into the business I said we can't just moisturize people—we have to begin to treat them. So we offered products that provided effective treatments for acne, pigmentation

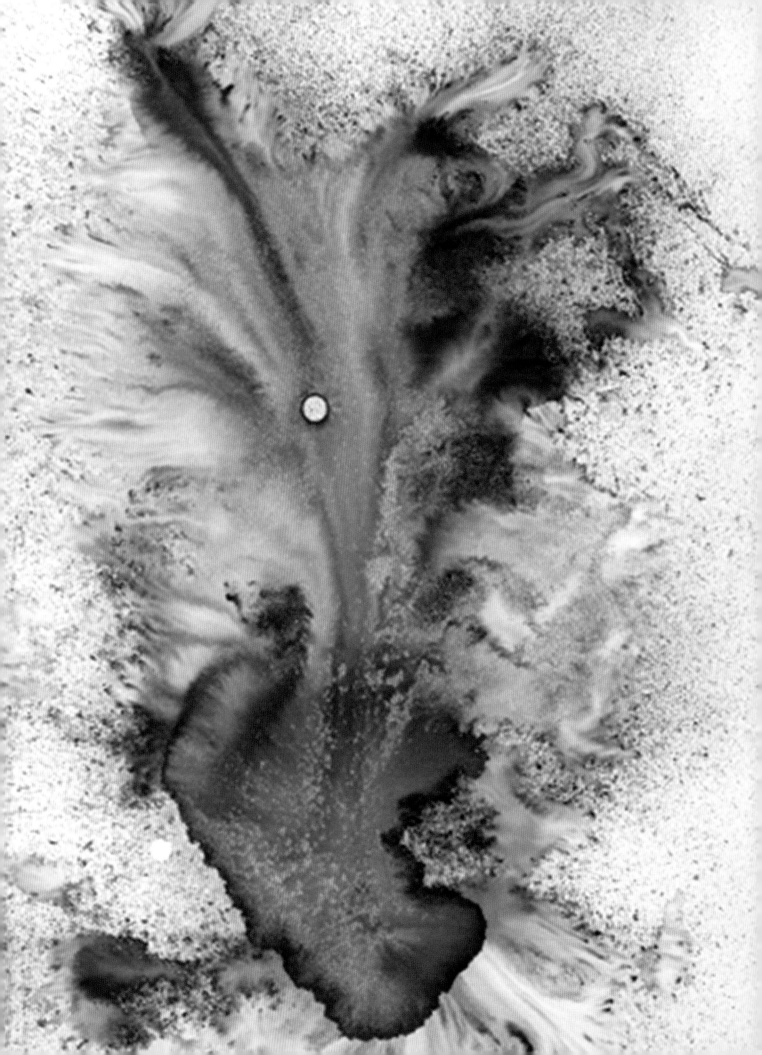

problems, wrinkles, and so on. In 1992 I started putting antioxidants and anti-inflammatories in all my products. In these ways and others, we set the trends rather than follow them. In general, we have set the trend for science-based treatments in the skincare industry.

I learned about these things—about what people need to take good care of their skin—from working with thousands of patients. What I learned from all those patients and from all that work, however, went much farther than skin deep. I learned, for instance, that what you eat has a powerful impact on how you look and the health of your skin. I also learned that the condition of your skin and your health in general is closely linked to cellular water—the hydration level of cells.

The Water Secret

We have trillions of cells in our bodies, and each one is connected either directly or indirectly to all the others. The health of any one cell influences the health of all the others, and the health of a cell depends on its ability to absorb and retain water. Every reasonable theory of aging points to one thing: water loss.

Your skin is drier today than it was ten years ago, and your cell membranes are also thinner and drier. Just as our skin protects our internal organs, the membrane protects the cell. Unfortunately, over time the cell membrane becomes thinner and thinner. Easily damaged, it becomes highly porous and begins to leak water, and when the cells dry out, they can't function.

As an analogy, think of an old-fashioned car battery. It had individual cells that wouldn't work unless they were filled with water. The chemicals needed to store electrical energy were all right there in the cells, but without water they were useless—the battery would die and the car wouldn't start. When the cells in our bodies lose water, they run down and die much like a car battery.

We know that certain stresses will damage cells and cause them to lose water. Exposure to sun, wind, and dry air as well as colds and the flu all cause us to lose water. A lot of water is lost through natural body processes such as the elimination of wastes, toxins, and microbes. Our livers detoxify the bad things we eat—and believe me, we eat lots of them—but the liver needs water to do its important work. Water is always part of the process. For instance, it takes 23 grams of water to eliminate just one gram of the salt we take in along with our food. We need salt, of course, but it is toxic when we get too much of it, and most people do have far too much salt in their diets.

Another way people lose water—and this tends to be ignored—is when they are under emotional stress. When you're under stress, you perspire. You have sweaty palms and so on, and you lose water that way. When you're under stress, your brain releases powerful chemicals that can damage the cell membranes, and this, too, causes water loss. Even low levels of stress, such as when you're standing in line at a store, can have a powerful negative effect on your health. The impact of low-level stress is cumulative, and this makes it even more damaging.

Our culture subjects us to nearly constant stress. Much of it is low-level stress hidden against the cluttered backdrop of our day-to-day lives, and we are not aware we are feeling it. I refer to this as *cultural stress*. For instance, when we fly we have to make sure we have the right shoes and that the bottles in our luggage aren't too large and that we get to the airport in time to get through security. These situations generate enormous stress. Traffic, air pollution, noise pollution, cells phones, email, complicated new computer programs—all these things cause stress, and at the same time, they isolate us from one another. We have less and less contact with friends and family, less and less personal contact of any kind with other human beings. We have contact through Facebook, text messages, and so on, but not much of the direct personal human contact we need to live healthy emotional lives. And our isolation itself causes stress.

Inclusive Health

How does a doctor treat patients who are bombarded with cultural stress, who are living increasingly isolated lives, and whose cells are dying of thirst? The traditional approach to medicine isn't the solution. Patients are unhealthy and unhappy, and their doctors aren't doing enough to help.

The number-one problem with medicine today is spot treatment—focusing on the disease or condition instead of the patient. We have new medicines, new equipment, and new everything, but even so, we're seeing more and more diabetes, more and more cancer, more and more depression. Why is that? Given all the innovations and the availability of sophisticated new treatments, shouldn't we be seeing less of these illnesses rather than more? Spot treatment, I believe, is

one important reason. What's needed is an approach that treats the patient rather than the disease. I call this approach *Inclusive Health.*

What separates Inclusive Health from other types of healthcare is understanding that the final common pathway of disease and aging is reduction in cellular water. When you are young and healthy, your cells are full of water. When you are sad, sick, or old, your cells contain less water. Inclusive Health is not just another version of preventive care, holistic care, or ayurvedic care. It's all of those, but the big difference is that it's all about the water. Inclusive Health is intended to prevent water loss in the cells and to increase the ability of cells to absorb and retain water.

The Inclusive Health approach consists of three main elements: external, internal, and emotional.

The *external* element involves protecting the skin from the sun, the weather, and harsh chemicals and improving its appearance through the use of appropriate skincare products. When you improve the appearance of your skin, you feel better about yourself, and when you are happy with the way you look, you are more likely to do the things that improve everything else about you.

The *internal* element is more or less a matter of what you eat. It addresses the water issue directly by adding water to the diet. It may come as a surprise to many, but drinking more water won't necessarily increase the hydration level of your cells. No doubt, you've heard that you should drink eight to ten glasses of water each day. You can do this if you wish, but much of that water is going to run right through you without being absorbed by the cells. Because cellular water must be absorbed slowly, the very best source of water is fresh fruit and vegetables. Those same fruits and vegetables are loaded with healthful vitamins, minerals, omega-3s, and fiber. So the message here is "eat your water!"

For most people, the *emotional* element of the Inclusive Health program is the most difficult one to put into practice. People tend to accumulate bad habits, and among the worst of these is the behavioral trap of thinking negative thoughts about themselves. If you are down on yourself, it's impossible to live a happy, healthy existence. The solution to this problem is to not think those thoughts—instead, be positive.

I've been listening to my patients for many years now, and they are their own harshest critics. In our society we are told we must strive for perfection. This may be intended to inspire excellence, but actually it is a prescription for failure. Perfection is impossible, and if everything we do must be perfect, how can we ever succeed? We try to be perfect, but we can't, and this makes us feel like failures.

Perfectionism is not the only source of negative thinking. Our up-to-date and up-to-the moment way of life generates an enormous amount of *cultural stress*. This type of stress is very damaging to our health, and we are all highly susceptible to it. Clocks and computers rule our lives, and so many different things are expected of us that we very commonly develop behaviors very much akin to those of attention deficit disorder. We read only the headlines and listen only to sound bites taken out of context and hope that will give us the essence of the content, but of course, it doesn't. As a result we feel increasingly detached from what's going on around us.

We also feel detached from one another. We spend hours on the phone but very little time at all in actual close contact with other people. We want to answer every voice message and respond to every one of the hundreds of emails we get each day. But we can't, and this makes us feel even more isolated and unworthy. These negative feelings make us increasingly unhappy and unhealthy.

Youth Building

To help my patients avoid all this negativity and feel better about themselves, I introduce them to a whole new way of thinking. Several years ago, I began to compile a list of sayings or insights—thoughts intended to help my patients take a fresh look at their lives. For instance: "Why have a bad day when you can have a good day?" That's one of the sayings, and in fact, it's the first one I actually wrote down.

Since then, the list of sayings has grown to more than 300, and it gets longer all the time. That's because I'm constantly seeing new patients. In one sense or another, each of the sayings comes from an experience I've had with a patient. Of course, the sayings are also heavily influenced by my own life experiences going all the way back to when I was a child living in New York.

The sayings play an essential role in the Inclusive Health treatment program. When I'm treating patients, I always share three or four of the sayings with them. You can never tell which of the sayings they are likely to find most meaningful, but they nearly always take one or another of them to heart. In this way they are reminded of what it takes to live a healthy life—for instance, eating a diet that emphasizes fresh fruits and vegetables. They are also reminded of what it takes to live a happy life. That doesn't mean living in luxury. It means taking a more youthful, creative attitude toward life itself. When people are introduced to these concepts, understand them, and begin to incorporate them into their lives, they don't just look younger, they act and feel younger, too. In essence, they *are* younger.

I call this *Youth Building,* and it is a fundamental element of my approach to medicine. Youth Building is a very different way of helping people deal with aging. Traditionally, doctors have concentrated on anti-aging techniques such as treatments for wrinkles, hair transplants, facelifts, and other cosmetic things intended to help people maintain their *appearance.* Those sorts of anti-aging techniques treat only the surface.

Youth Building functions at a much deeper level. It not only helps you look better but also restores youth. It is intended to make all cells in your body as healthy as possible and protect them from damage. It also enables you to live and interact with the world the way you did when you were younger, when you were not so worried about what others were thinking about you. Incidentally, that sort of thinking has already set in by the age of two.

Youth Building is about acting the way you did when you felt completely free from the scrutiny of others, free to take risks, and free to put your fingers in the paint and get messy, so to speak. It's about being willing to enjoy life and go wherever it takes you, about a willingness to look at your surroundings and the world itself with fresh eyes—not unlike the way a two-year-old might look at it. If you can do those things, you can limit or reverse the damage caused by cultural stress.

In a way, the art I create describes me and my philosophy on life and medicine. What the art teacher in Ojai said to me turned out to be true. You don't need classes to learn art. You can learn from yourself. All that's required is your natural creativity and a need for self-expression. And what's true of art is also true of life. The canvas is your life. Just take a little paint and get started.

Dr. Howard Murad's
INSPIRATIONAL INSIGHTS AND ART

DR. HOWARD MURAD'S
INSPIRATIONAL INSIGHTS AND ART

Through in-depth research and experience with thousands of patients, Dr. Murad has developed a unique approach to healthcare. It is based on his realization that good health—or the lack of it—is determined by the hydration levels of cells throughout the body. This medical breakthrough was articulated in an earlier book published in 2010 by John Wiley & Sons under the title *The Water Secret*.

Dr. Murad's approach is also driven by his conviction that doctors should treat *people*, not diseases. In line with this concept—endorsed by a growing number of other prominent physicians and internationally recognized experts—he has composed a substantial collection of inspirational sayings or insights. Dr. Murad shares these brief meditations with patients to help them improve their health by adopting more youthful, creative, and health-conscious lifestyles.

In *The Water Secret,* Dr. Murad recommends eating raw fruits and vegetables with high moisture content rather than bother too much about drinking the recommended six to eight glasses of water daily. *The Water Secret* devotes the better part of 60,000 words to this innovative concept. In his sayings, however, Dr. Murad manages to boil it down to just three words: *Eat your water.* Most of his sayings are like that; they are highly concentrated aphorisms delivering bits of health advice, philosophy, and wisdom straight up, like strong coffee.

Generally speaking, his sayings are things people already know but rarely, if ever, consider. For instance, you must *give yourself permission to be happy.*

"Some people experience very little happiness in their lives," says Dr. Murad. "They don't believe they are supposed to be happy. They're waiting for someone to give them permission to be happy, but of course, happiness doesn't require anyone's permission."

Others may be waiting for someone to give them permission to be successful. Of course, they don't need that; instead, success will come only if you are prepared to take chances. *Success comes when you accept the possibility of failure.*

Don't measure yourself against unattainable goals, he says, and recognize your own imperfection. *Be imperfect, live longer.* If you do these things, you'll have far more self-confidence and live a happier, healthier life. You'll be a more likeable person, too, and you'll have more friends.

These and many similar sayings have become a regular feature of Dr. Murad's medical practice, and they are a primary means he uses to treat the whole person rather than a condition or disease.

"A positive state of mind and emotional well-being are necessary for good health," he says. "I find the sayings help my patients have a more positive outlook, which then becomes part of their treatment." Dr. Murad often composes a new saying to fit the circumstances and needs of an individual patient. For this reason the number of his sayings grows practically daily. Readers will almost certainly receive help and inspiration from the more than 300 sayings found throughout *Creating a Healthy Life* or in the comprehensive list beginning on page 123.

Many of the most popular sayings have been paired with pieces of art created by the author himself. Dr. Murad considers self-expression as essential to human health and happiness as what people eat or how they live, and several years ago he found a new outlet for his own irrepressible creative drive: painting. Interestingly enough, he's never taken any formal art classes, but his canvases are nonetheless sophisticated. His modernist style makes pure chance a key element in the creative process. This results in explosions of color and form that expand the limits of imagination.

Dr. Murad says he lives much the way he paints—or perhaps it is the other way around. "Life is a canvas, you see. Make your mark on the canvas and then flow with it. If you allow it to flow in a way that makes sense to you, your life will be a work of art."

Why have a bad day when you can have a good day?

Having a wonderful day or a terrible day is less a matter of circumstances than it is of choice. You can choose to have a good day—or not. It's entirely up to you. This may be the most important of the sayings or simple truths you'll encounter in this book, and it's the heart of my philosophy. Always try to focus on good things instead of negative ones.

"Even in disaster, look for the good."

"Think positive; detoxify your brain."

"Rewrite and reframe the negatives in your life."

"Life is good, bad, and indifferent—
focus on the good."

Smile daily,
frown infrequently.

When you smile, you're focusing on the positive, and when people see you smile, they're likely to believe you are a positive person. When you frown, the opposite is true. You're focused on negative things and likely to make a negative impression on others. Smile often and you just might find there are a lot of good reasons to keep smiling.

"Project happiness."

"Project loving and caring."

"Embrace health."

"You have no control over
the cards that are dealt to you.
But you do have control
of how you play them."

Murad

Surround yourself with happiness.

If you place yourself in a happy environment, you are much more likely to experience happiness. It's much easier to be happy in a room full of happy people than in a room full of people who are miserable.

"Make your house your home."

"Heal yourself, reduce isolation."

"Share your love."

"Bear hugs keep the doctor away."

Happiness does not require luxury.

Luxurious surroundings are nice, if you can afford them, but they won't make you happy. Think back. Was your happiest birthday dinner the one at the fanciest restaurant? Or was it a simpler one you shared with close friends and family gathered around the kitchen table?

"Think of yourself as royalty,
not poverty."

"Begin to know exactly what you want."

"Developing your passion is a major
step along the journey to happiness."

"Be thankful."

"You will be most happy
when your loved ones are happy."

Increase simplicity in your life.

Appointments, deadlines, emails, and cell phone calls—most of us make our daily lives far too complicated. The complexity of modern life causes cultural stress, which, in turn, makes us unhappy and sick. To reduce cultural stress and improve your health, look for ways to simplify your life. You will discover that you can live very simply— and very well.

*"Don't set yourself up for
    unrealistic expectations."*

"Unify a diverse message."

"Take pleasure in every minor success."

"Choose the best environment for you."

Reduce complexity in your life.

Complexity breeds stress and may be preventing you from reaching your goals. Simplify your daily life, and you may discover that you are capable of far more than you ever thought possible.

*"Reduce the number of decisions
you have to make each day."*

"Reduce Internet isolation; sleep better."

"Be more efficient—reduce waist."

"Expect less, be happy."

Don't focus on
the minutia in life.

You've heard the adage that "he can't see the forest for the trees." If you get too caught up in the details of life, you'll lose sight of the bigger, more important things. Keep in mind that success in almost any endeavor requires you to see the big picture and grasp the full sweep of events.

*"Focus on your ultimate goals
and not the steps getting there."*

*"If you put what you are worrying about in
perspective, it's probably no big deal."*

"Don't sweat the small stuff."

*"When you come to a wall in the road,
life is telling you to make a turn."*

Be imperfect, live longer.

Our modern culture places so many demands on us that we cannot keep up with them all. We think there are schedules we have to keep, meetings we have to attend, places we have to go, things we have to buy—it's just too much, and we know it, but we still try to get everything done. We feel we must be perfect in every way, but of course, we can't, and this makes us feel like failures.

By striving for perfection, we damage ourselves both psychologically and physically. Being hard on yourself all the time makes you unhappy, and unhappiness causes your brain to release chemicals that damage your cells. It doesn't have to be that way. You may not be able to answer every email the hour you receive it. But that's okay! Accept the fact that you are imperfect, and you'll live a happier, healthier, and longer life.

"Beware of creating your own stress."

"Don't be so hard on yourself."

"Be thrilled with who you are."

"Your harshest critic may have become you yourself."

Aging is a fact of life.
Looking your age is not.

We now understand that lifestyle plays an important role in preventing and treating many types of disease. A healthy lifestyle is also the key to looking and feeling much younger. If you modify your lifestyle by eating better, reducing stress (particularly cultural stress), staying out of the sun, putting appropriate products on your skin, and living a happier life, you'll look a lot younger.

You can't stop the clock. None of us can. You can't change the fact that you've gotten a year older than you were last year. But you don't have to look like you're a year older. Even if you are 90 years old, you don't have to look 90. Looking your age or looking much younger is a matter of choice. It's up to you.

"Lifestyle can modify genes."

"Restore youth."

"Live young."

"Turn the rest of your life into the best of your life."

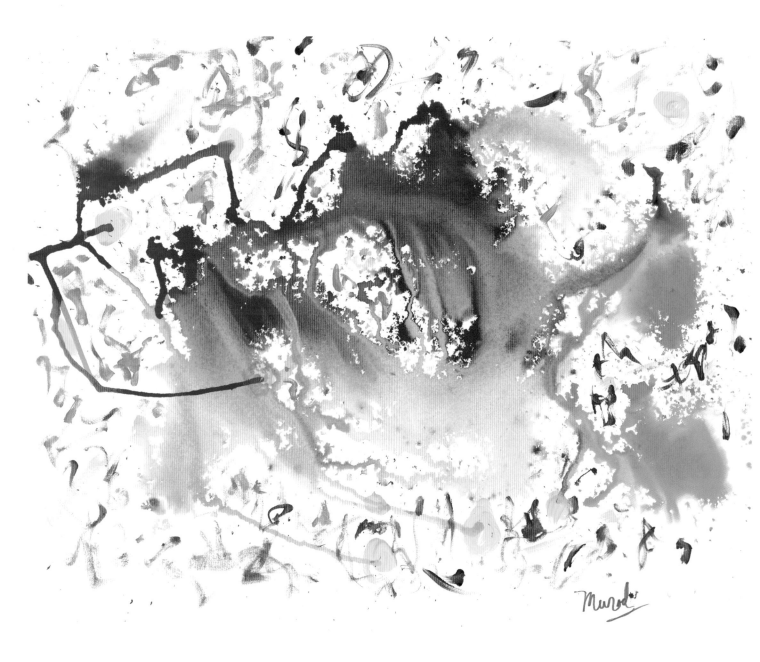

Healthy skin is a reflection of overall wellness.

Healthy skin is not just a matter of appearances. Your skin is connected to every organ in your body. Generally speaking, when your skin looks good, chances are the rest of your body is basically healthy. Good skincare is also good healthcare.

"Not just the science but the art of health."

"Expect to be healthy."

"Think healthy."

"Be imperfect—get better skin and fewer blemishes."

Healthy, hydrated cells are the key to ageless skin and a healthy body.

Scientific research, including our own work with more than 4,000 individual patients, has shown a direct link between good health and high levels of cellular water. Basically, the more you increase your cellular water, the healthier you will become. The opposite is also true. When you lose cellular water, you open the door to aging and disease.

"Water loss is the final common pathway to all aging and disease."

"Improve your genes."

"Without healing there is no health."

"Reduce stress to increase total body hydration."

Before there was medicine there was food.

If you ate well, you wouldn't need so much medicine. A major health concern in this society is our food, which is said to contain too many calories, too much fat, and too little real nutrition. I believe a far more important issue is how much—or how little—water is found in the foods we eat. Most of our food is too dry. It contains very little of the moisture required to keep our cells well hydrated and healthy. It is often said that people are overfed and undernourished. I say we're overfed and underhydrated.

"Before there was surgery, there was Inclusive Health."

"Medicine is imperfect; you have to look at it inclusively."

"Find elements of health from around the world."

"Before there was medicine there was food. Before there was food there was chocolate!"

Eat your water.

You've probably heard you should drink eight glasses of water a day. Unfortunately, that won't do much to improve your health. If you drink that much water, it'll just run right through you without adding any of the critical moisture your cells need to survive. To properly hydrate your cells, you need to eat raw fruits and vegetables. They contain lots of structural water that is slowly absorbed into the body. These same raw fruits and vegetables also contain healthful antioxidants and roughage to eliminate fat and help your body resist bone loss and cancer.

"Understand the source of healthy nutrition."

"The ultimate cellular need is water."

"Detoxify your body with plants."

"Eat your medicine."

"Water-rich foods—the best diet plan."

Return to your youth.

To look good, feel good, stay healthy, and achieve your goals, maintain a youthful attitude throughout your life. Rather than trying to fight the aging process, focus on Youth Building. This means doing the things you did when you were young—and doing them the way you did them then—in the same youthful spirit. Youth springs from within.

"Allow spontaneity in your life."

"Youth Building—the path to positive self-talk."

"Learn who you really are."

"Be yourself, don't emulate."

Give yourself an opportunity to have a transformation.

Most of the key positive changes in our lives come about as the result of personal transformations. These transformations don't just happen by themselves. We have to be open to them and to all the possibilities they represent.

"Evolve quickly to reach your goal."

"Start a revolution."

"The largest explosion starts with
a few grains of sand."

"Your life's story is based on you developing it."

"Allow yourself to take a chance."

Give yourself permission to be happy.

Some people experience very little happiness in their lives because they don't believe they are supposed to be happy. They're waiting for someone to give them permission to be happy. Happiness does not require a permit, and you don't need anyone's permission. You can and *should* give it to yourself.

"Become yourself."

"Allow happiness to enter."

"There is a difference between
having fun and being happy."

"Honor yourself."

Happiness means finding beauty every day.

There's beauty everywhere, and if you take the time to notice it, you will find it all around you. When you're looking for beauty, you're not focusing on the negative, and that will make you healthier and happier.

"When going along the path of life,
                                   always look up."

"Find beauty everywhere."

"Heal yourself; allow the unique you to blossom."

"Don't deal with what you could have done.
                   *Deal with what you are **going** to do."*

Magic only happens when you create your own.

Like works of art, loving relationships involve a sort of magic. No one else can bring that magic into your life; only you can do it, because the magic must come from within. A friend or loved one can help, but you'll experience those special magical moments only when you are open to them and you create the conditions that make them possible.

"Explore your hidden opportunities."

*"Embrace the little things you do;
          they may really be big things."*

"The privilege of making your own decisions."

*"We are each born with a unique commodity
          called life. It is stressed by the environment,
          and it is up to us to make the best of it."*

Be interested so you can become interesting.

If you don't take an interest in the world and the people around you, how can you expect them to be interested in you? You can complain that you have no friends or that nobody seems to like you, but if you can't talk intelligently about anything, what can you expect? Explore the fascinating universe of ideas, events, art, science, and nature. Demonstrate a passion for life, and the world will take notice.

"Isolation can be a self-imposed prison."

"Take each day as an opportunity to grow."

"Remember to wear your crown."

"Find education wherever it resides."

You are worthy.

A strong sense of personal worthiness is the key to health, happiness, and success. Unless you feel worthy of success, you won't experience it. Unless you feel worthy of love, you are unlikely to receive it. You are worthy and you should remind yourself of that continually.

"Feel that you are about to improve—and you will."

"When you are comfortable with yourself,
your accomplishments will amaze you."

"Be someone special."

"Be too big for your britches."

Become free to be yourself.

Trying to copy others won't help you become the person you were meant to be. What's wrong with being that genuine and capable person you really are? Everybody has something unique to contribute. Celebrate yourself and what you have to offer.

"Find your hidden potential."

"Develop your unique power."

"Progress starts when you cut the umbilical cord."

"Just be."

"The privilege of doing purposeful work."

Expose your accomplishments to others without fear of rejection.

Share your achievements with others without being afraid of how they're going to respond. Likely they'll appreciate what you've achieved and will celebrate it with you. If not, you still have a right to take pride in what you've accomplished.

"Project self-confidence."

"Be brave enough to expose yourself to your harshest critic."

"Follow your path despite what others think."

"Let yourself speak."

Be brave enough to make difficult decisions.

Decisions—since they involve choices that may turn out to be either right or wrong—can be very difficult. Sometimes we avoid decisions because we're afraid of making the wrong one. But making no decision at all can be even worse. Decisions have to be made all the time, and avoiding them will paralyze you. Decision-making takes guts, but you'll never make the right decision unless you're brave enough to take a chance on getting it wrong. To succeed, you must have the courage to fail.

"Turn transitions into an opportunity for positive changes."

"Failure is the path to success."

"When making a difficult decision, solitude is a necessary element."

The road to success runs through managing change.

What's the most constant thing in life? It's change. You have to be able to manage that change if you want to be successful. If gas prices get too high, maybe it's time to look for an alternative fuel.

"Make sure you can buy gas before you buy a car."

"Don't let the vagaries lead to vacancies."

"Technology can turn the impossible into the possible."

"Life always throws curve balls— learn to hit them out of the park."

Sometimes one key can open many doors.

Often a single solution can solve many different problems. This is especially true in the health field, where one disease can have multiple symptoms that will fade away when the illness itself is cured. The same is often true in our personal and professional lives. Many troubles may stem from a single central cause. Correct that problem and the others will be fixed along with it.

"Find your direction and focus on it."

"Look for what you can't find;
it may actually be in front of your eyes."

"Look out of the box for solutions
to your problems."

"When life looks bleak, look for
a window for change."

Don't measure yourself against unattainable goals.

You'll probably never run a two-minute mile, swim the width of the Pacific, or be the richest person in the world. It's very unhelpful and unhealthful to measure yourself against goals that are either unattainable or out of the realm of possibility. In fact, it's usually best not to measure yourself against the achievements of others. Instead, set reasonable goals of your own and measure yourself against those.

"If you can't find it, you may be looking
for the wrong thing."

"Many short-cuts turn into long-cuts."

"Become a champion in your own league."

"Think of the endgame.

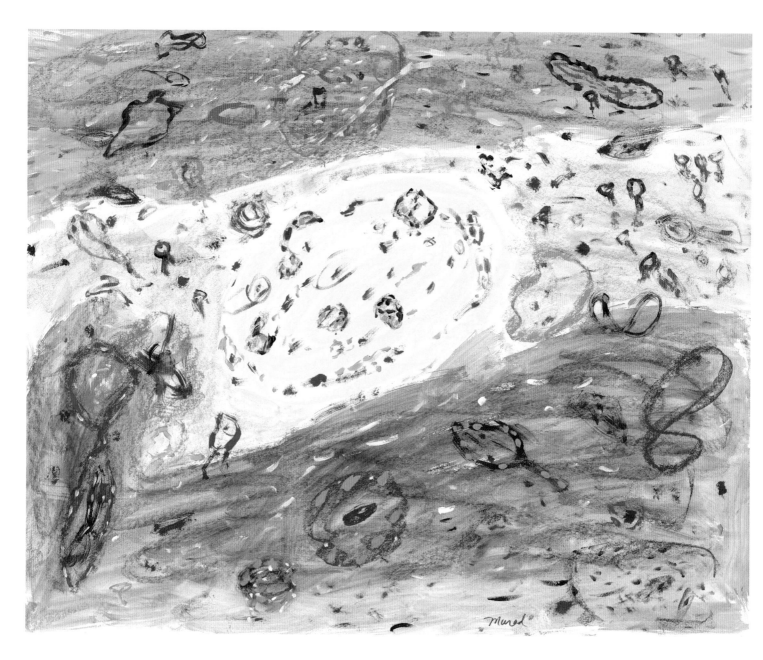

Perfectionism leads to pessimism.

We try to be perfect but, of course, this is the real world and perfection is impossible. When we strive for perfection we are bound to fail. And failure leads to pessimism, because it makes us think we don't measure up—that we're not good enough to succeed. Naturally, you want to do whatever you do as well as you can. But strive for excellence, not perfection.

"In order to reach your potential you
must risk failure."

"Opportunity changes luck."

"When you learn to be imperfect,
your life will be more perfect."

"Positive self-talk encourages a positive outcome."

Have only big, flexible dreams with no limits so that your potential will have no limits.

All too often we focus on narrow, limited goals such as buying a new car or getting a promotion when what we really should be seeking is a complete change in our approach to life. Instead of pursuing a promotion, perhaps you should consider going into a whole new field or profession.

"You can catch more fish with a net than a hook."

"Make the best of transitions in your life."

"Success comes when you don't fear failure."

"You never know until you try."

Make your journey without a destination.

Don't get caught up in goals and objectives that are too specific. Be open to changing course when necessary and taking advantage of opportunities as they present themselves.

"Move before the ceiling gets too low."

"Accept the potential for the unexpected."

"Take others along the path with you."

"Realistic expectations can go beyond what you are theoretically entitled to."

Invent the future today.

We never gain much ground by repeating the failures—or even the successes—of the past. Open yourself to fresh ideas and experiences that lead you into unexplored regions. That way you'll learn completely new things that will enable you to create a brighter future.

"Inspiration before perspiration."

"Stay ahead of the curve even though it is a lonely journey."

"Make trailblazing a way of life."

"Before there was a revolution, there was an evolution."

Success comes when you accept the possibility of failure.

If you fail, just pick yourself up and try again. A single instance of failure—even a thousand such failures—need not spell defeat. Don't be afraid of failure. Just keep on trying, because if you don't try, you'll never succeed.

"Fear of failure leads to failure."

*"If you haven't failed,
                    you haven't really succeeded."*

*"Give yourself permission
                    to be successful."*

"Delete negative self-talk."

Think of it as an opportunity when your expectations are not met.

Failure in one venture may lead to success in others. If you lose your job or don't get that raise you were expecting, you can complain or pout about it all you want, but it won't get you anywhere. Why not instead treat an apparent failure as an opportunity? Who knows where it may lead you? When engineering school didn't work out for me, I decided to go to pharmacy school. This led me into medicine, which turned out to have been the right field for me all along. Give yourself a chance to be lucky.

"Don't let failures spoil your success."

"Opportunity comes to those who ask."

"Don't set yourself up
*   for unrealistic expectations."*

"Accept the potential for the unexpected."

Competency trumps genius.

Competence often succeeds where genius, for one reason or another, may fail. You don't have to be a genius to succeed or to accomplish great things.

"Attitude trumps intelligence."

"Handouts may turn into holdouts."

"Your competitive advantage is
doing your best."

"Resolution requires concentration."

Your best is better than the competition.

Doing your very best is likely to make you a winner. Concentrate on those talents and abilities that are the very best you have to offer. There is always something you are better at than anyone else.

"Be comfortable with who you are."

"You are valuable; don't sell yourself short."

"Lead yourself."

"Learn from others but establish your own journey."

Give yourself permission to say **no.**

No is a very powerful word, and it is okay to say it. In fact, the right to say *no* is what makes us sovereign individuals. You don't always have to do what other people say. You can say *no* and make up your own mind about what you're going to do.

"When you become the most important person to yourself, your accomplishments will amaze you."

"Give yourself permission to make changes in your life when appropriate."

"Give yourself permission to have your own opinion."

"Give yourself permission to be loved."

If it's not personal, don't take it personally.

Our day-to-day lives are filled with stress—traffic jams, long lines, emails, cell phone messages, and an endless swirl of things that demand our attention. This sort of cultural clutter often leads to a type of attention deficit disorder. All we can absorb are sound bites. We read only a few lines at the beginning of a news article and we don't get the whole story. Because of all this confusion, we begin to take things personally that are not personal in any way.

"If it is no big deal, don't make a big deal about it."

"Reality, not rhetoric."

"Replace cultural stress and negative self-talk with a positive attitude."

"Understand the real reason for your decisions."

Accommodate but don't let your life turn upside down.

It's often necessary to accommodate others and consider their needs and requests. However, you must never carry the process of accommodation to the point that you lose sight of your own needs. Be your own person.

"Accommodate but maintain your power."

"Accommodate but don't be disconnected."

"Accommodate but realize what you are doing."

"Don't become used and abused."

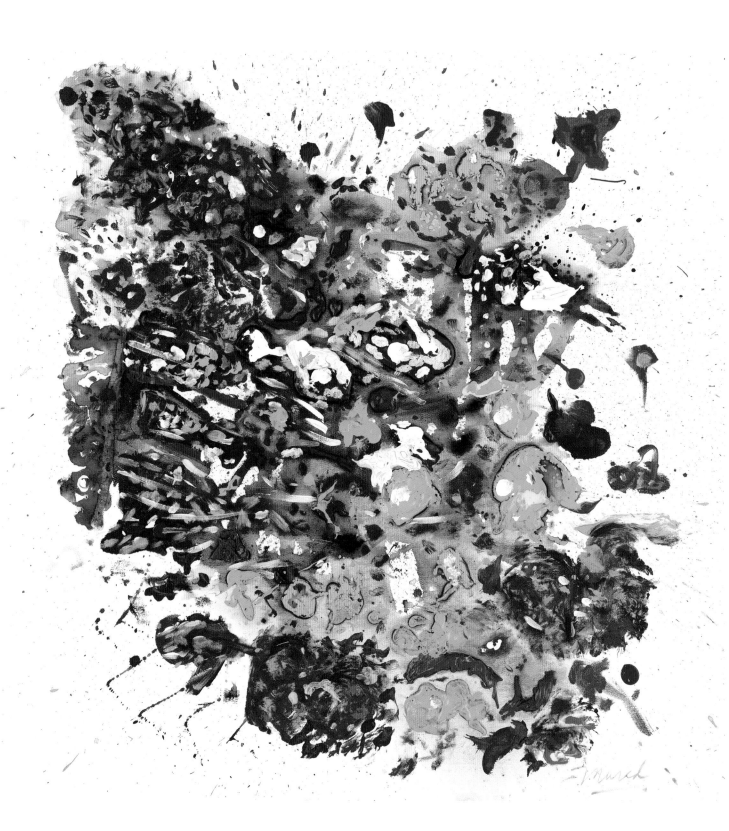

Survive despite being damaged.

Life confronts us with a lot of bumps, and over the years we all get bruised in one way or another. Sometimes the damage is severe. But no matter how heartbreaking the loss, we have to keep on going. Even after the worst fires, forests sooner or later turn green again.

"Be stable during times of instability."

"When you fall down, get up quickly."

"Transitions are imperfect road maps to the future. It is up to you to make the best of them."

"Think of transition as an opportunity."

"Handouts don't always pay out."

See sunshine in gray skies.

Always think positive thoughts and do positive things. No matter how difficult life may become—no matter how gray and dreary the sky may appear—you can find bright patches of sunshine if you look for them.

"During times of darkness, look for illusions of light and warmth."

"Color darkness with bright colors."

"Try laughter when you are in pain."

"Failure comes when you don't try."

"Become free."

Learn from your mistakes.
Don't project them on others.

It's easy to complain about somebody else and, in this way, avoid taking responsibility for your own mistakes. That's a very destructive way of dealing with problems. You get no benefit from this and neither does anybody else. Instead of projecting responsibility on others, accept it yourself.

"Don't blame your second-grade teacher
for your failures."

"Many different problems have the same solution."

"Begin to know when it is enough."

"If you keep banging your head against the wall,
you will have a headache, no matter how many
pain relievers you take."

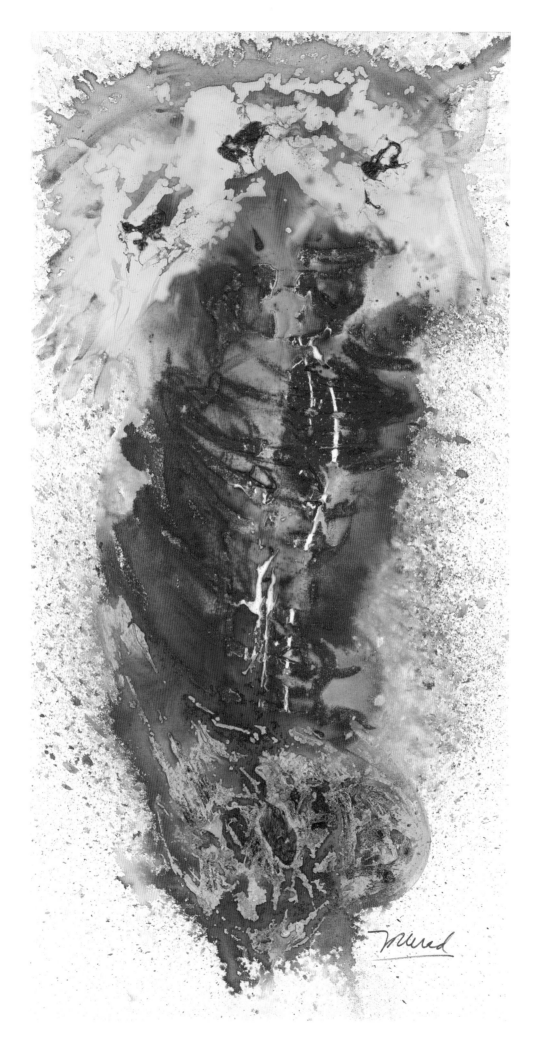

Stay in touch
with your passion.

Far too many of us don't know our own hearts. We've either forgotten or never even discovered what truly motivates and excites us. Make believe you had nothing to do tomorrow and ask yourself how you would spend the day. More people than you may think say they would use the day to catch up on sleep. There's nothing wrong with getting a little extra sleep—most of us are sleep deprived, after all. But why not use the time for something you really love? Take a drive into the mountains, or spend some pleasant hours with an art project, reading, or interacting with others. You may never know what your real passion is until you give it a chance to thrive.

"Be friends with your passion."

"Enjoy intimacy."

*"Go for it, no matter how unattainable
it may seem."*

"Allow your true passion to enter."

"Give yourself permission to have a passion."

Free those you love.

When you love others, don't build walls around them. Instead, open doors for them and encourage them to become themselves and to do the things that bring them joy. In some wedding ceremonies, the young couple is encouraged to "grow apart together." That's a wonderful formula for a deep and loving long-term relationship.

*"When you are smitten, it is important
to maintain your own persona."*

"Be comfortable in yourself to free others."

"Encourage healing."

"Let others help you by taking the first step."

"Be happy when you see happiness in others."

Happiness resides within.

Material things can't make you happy. Neither can other people. Whether you are happy or not depends on whether you are open to the happiness that flows from within.

"To be happy, don't measure yourself against others."

"Become a champion in your own division."

"Eat to hydrate your brain, allowing happiness to enter."

"Inhibitions increase with age, so stay young."

Think of your life
as a vacation.

One day an associate asked me about my vacation plans. "I don't know," I replied somewhat jokingly. "My life is a vacation."

Later when I thought about it, I realized that this is true. I feel like I'm on vacation just about every day, and I wouldn't have it any other way. Life should always be that way. If it's drudgery or if it's boring, you should make some changes.

When you go on vacation you look at things that you never saw before and do things for the sheer joy of doing them. Your life should be like that all the time. A vacation is thought of as an opportunity for relaxation, regeneration, and reflection, but you need those things constantly, not just once or twice a year.

"Splurge often."

"Treat yourself as royalty."

*"It's not the stress—it is how
you respond to it."*

"Don't wait to do the bucket list."

Your life's story, in the end, is how you have lived it. Make it sweet, happy, and healthy.

Your life is like a novel, and you are the novelist. In the end, only you can write your life's story, and how you write it is entirely up to you.

*"Develop a basic recipe for your healthy life
and allow it to be modified over time."*

*"Wherever you are on life's journey, there is an
opportunity for positive change."*

*"Make additions rather than deletions
to your lifestyle."*

*"To reach your full potential, live in a
healthy physical and emotional environment."*

Make your mark but allow the canvas of life to direct you.

When I paint, I make a few marks on a canvas, add some colors, and then allow the water spray to interact with them. This often carries the artwork in a totally unexpected direction. How's it going to turn out? I don't know.

My life has been like that too. I started out thinking I wanted to be an engineer. When that didn't work out, I went into pharmacy, and that, in turn, led me into medicine. Whatever happened along the way, I always felt life was carrying me somewhere.

Life is a canvas, you see. You make your mark on it and then flow with it. If you allow it to flow in a way that makes sense, your life will be a work of art.

"Watch for random events
that can change your life."

"Allow transitions to have
a powerful impact on you."

"The best is yet to come; you just have
to let it enter."

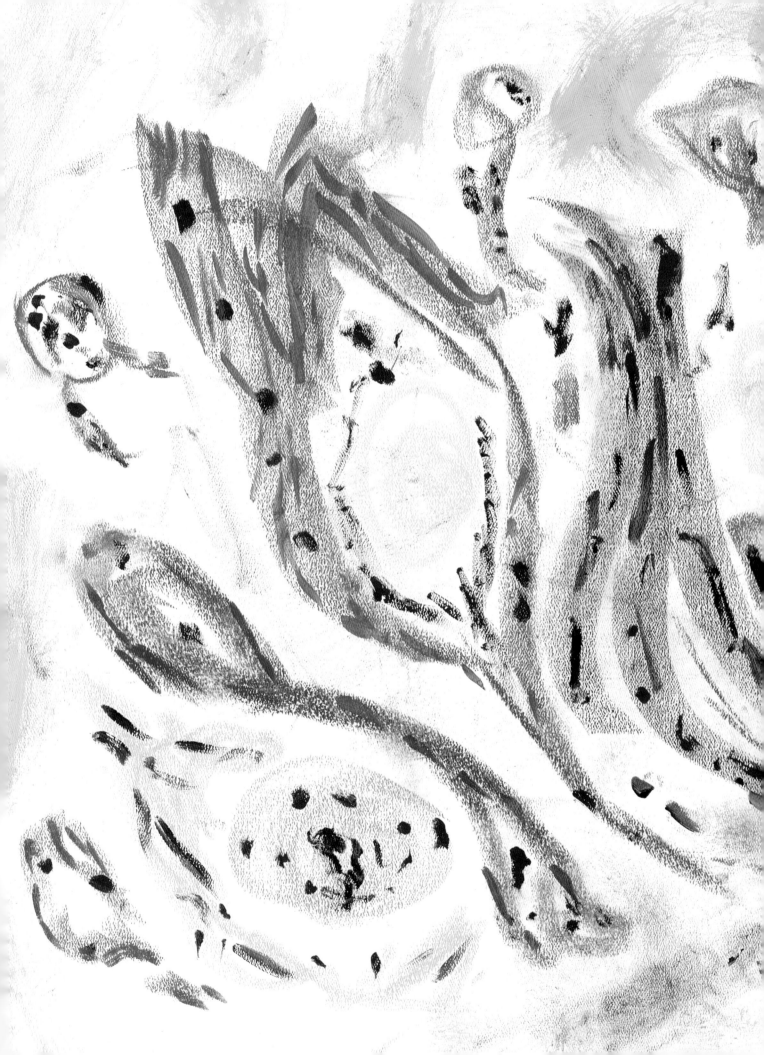

Index of Sayings

The following is a complete list of the sayings that Dr. Murad shares with patients. While the list is comprehensive at present, it grows constantly as his life experience and medical practice inspire fresh insights. You have encountered many of these sayings earlier in this book, but there are many others here that you may find interesting or useful in your daily life. The sayings are listed in the same order they occurred to him.

Why have a bad day when you can have a good day?

Before there was medicine, there was food.

Aging is a fact of life. Looking your age is not.

Healthy skin is a reflection of overall wellness.

Healthy, hydrated cells are the key to ageless skin and a healthy body.

We are each born with a unique commodity called life. It is stressed by the environment, and it is up to us to make the best of it.

When you come to a wall in the road, life is telling you to make a turn.

You have no control over the cards that are dealt to you. But you do have control of how you play them.

Magic only happens when you create your own.

Be comfortable with who you are.

Be imperfect, live longer.

Learn from the vagaries of life.

Even in disaster, look for the good.

Smile daily, frown infrequently.

Look out of the box for solutions to your problems.

Happiness resides within.

Before there was surgery, there was Inclusive Health.

Don't let failures spoil your success.

Ignore the naysayers from without and, more importantly, those from within. Allow

yourself to achieve your maximum potential.

Have only big, flexible dreams with no limits so that your potential will have no limits.

Be too big for your britches.

The healing power of pride.

Lead yourself.

Stay in touch with your passion.

Don't let vagaries lead to vacancies.

Stay ahead of the curve even though it is a lonely journey.

Allow spontaneity in your life.

Equal parts vegetables and vegging out keeps the doctor away.

The largest explosion starts with a few grains of sand.

123

Eighty percent of health resides in the brain.

Eat your water.

Be friends with passion.

If it's not personal, don't take it personally.

Turn the rest of your life into the best of your life.

Isolation can be a self-imposed prison.

When the ceiling gets too low, it's time to move.

Take pleasure in every minor success.

The best is yet to come; you just have to let it enter.

Explore your hidden opportunities.

Find your hidden potential.

Water loss is the final common pathway to all aging and disease.

Make trailblazing a way of life.

Be more efficient— reduce waist.

Rewrite and reframe the negatives in your life.

Reduce Internet isolation; sleep better.

Let others help you.

Splurge often.

In order to learn, ask yourself before asking others.

Life is good, bad, and indifferent—focus on the good.

Feel that you are about to improve—and you will.

Evolve quickly to reach your goal.

Learn from your disability.

Live young.

When going along the path of life, always look up.

Many short-cuts turn into long-cuts.

Die late, not old.

Before there was a revolution, there was an evolution.

Resolution requires concentration.

Be consistent with your message, but be flexible enough to be transformed.

Increase simplicity in your life.

Reduce complexity in your life.

Be thrilled with who you are.

Make your house your home.

Listen to yourself so you can pay attention to your needs.

Unify a diverse message.

Reduce the number of decisions you have to make each day.

When making a difficult decision, solitude is a necessary element.

Transformation can happen in 12 weeks.

Take each day as an opportunity to grow.

Share your love.

Inclusive Health reduces waist.

The Water Secret is the unifying method of reducing aging, disease, and wrinkles.

Progress starts when you cut the umbilical cord.

Success comes by cutting your own umbilical cords and allowing freedom.

Medicine is imperfect; you have to look at it inclusively.

Surround yourself with happiness.

Bear hugs keep the doctor away.

Enjoy intimacy.

Index of Sayings

The healing power of love.

Find elements of health from around the world.

The healing power of water.

Take others along the path with you.

Treat yourself as royalty.

The ultimate cellular need is water.

Opportunities abound. Keep your eyes open for them.

Expect less, be happy.

Make additions rather than deletions to your lifestyle.

Detoxify your body with plants.

Improve your immunity with plants.

Think positive; detoxify your brain.

Start a revolution.

Reality, not rhetoric.

If you can't find it, you may be looking for the wrong thing.

When you fall down, get up quickly.

Be someone special.

Find your direction and focus on it.

Heal yourself, reduce isolation.

Opportunity comes to those who.

Perfectionism leads to pessimism.

There is a difference between having fun and being happy.

Be brave enough to make difficult decisions.

When you become the most important person to yourself, your accomplishments will amaze you.

Make Inclusive Health your destiny.

The privilege of making your own decisions.

The privilege of doing purposeful work.

Be stable during times of instability.

Failure is the path to success.

Don't be so hard on yourself.

Beware of creating your own stress.

Inclusive Health—the no-diet weight loss plan.

Water is necessary for cell function.

If you haven't failed, you haven't really succeeded.

Look for what you can't find; it may actually be in front of your eyes.

Don't wait to do the bucket list.

Not just the science but the art of health.

Competency trumps genius.

Cultural stress equals Attention Deficit Hyperactivity Disorder (ADHD).

Cultural stress equals dependency and addiction.

Attitude trumps intelligence.

Learn from your mistakes. Don't project them on others.

If you put what you are worrying about in perspective, it's probably no big deal.

When you are smitten, it is important to maintain your own persona.

Don't become used and abused.

Lifestyle can modify genes.

Embellish your genes.

Improve your genes.

Make your mark but allow the canvas of life to direct you.

Allow happiness to enter.

Replenish your passion.

Restore youth.

You are valuable; don't sell yourself short.

When you learn to be imperfect, your life will be more perfect.

Technology can turn the impossible into the possible.

Create a competitive advantag Your best is better than the competition.

Your competitive advantage is doing your best.

Failure comes when you don't try.

Success comes when you try.

Fear of failure leads to failure.

Success comes when you don't fear failure.

Success comes when you accept the possibility of failure.

Go for it, no matter how unattainable it may seem.

It may just be your turn.

Believe you are good enough for...

Watch for random events that can change your life.

Return to your youth.

Begin to know exactly what you want.

Think of yourself as royalty, not poverty.

Give yourself permission to have your own opinion.

Give yourself permission to be happy.

Give yourself permission to make changes in your life when appropriate.

In order to reach your potential you must risk failure.

Opportunity changes luck.

Open yourself to an opportunity for a chance to be lucky.

Don't measure yourself against unattainable goals.

To be happy, don't measure yourself against others.

Don't set yourself up for unrealistic expectations.

Survive despite being damaged.

If permitted, failure leads to success.

Before there was medicine there was food. Before there was food there was chocolate.

Give yourself permission to say no.

You are worthy.

Expose your accomplishments to others without fear of rejection.

Accept the potential for the unexpected.

Accommodate but don't let your life turn upside down.

Accommodate but maintain your power.

Accommodate but realize what you are doing.

Accommodate but expect to be recognized for it.

Accommodate but don't be disconnected.

Become yourself.

Be heard.

Be thankful.

Be interested.

Project happiness.

Project self-confidence.

Index of Sayings

Happiness means finding beauty every day.

Inspiration before perspiration.

Wait for the big fish that loves you by making yourself better while you wait.

The message can always be massaged depending on the messenger's point of view.

If you want to be miserable every day, you will find something that went wrong even if 99 percent went right.

Give yourself permission to...

Accept the possibility that your expectations won't be met.

Think of it as an opportunity when your expectations are not met.

Be interested so you can become interesting.

When you have intentions to.... it is more likely to happen.

Understand the real reason for your decisions.

When medical therapy exposes your body to a new environment, take it as an opportunity for a positive change.

To address life's ever-increasing fast-paced changes, you need to be flexible.

Don't focus on the minutia in life.

Healing is central to health.

Make your journey without a destination.

Happiness does not require luxury.

Think of your life as a vacation.

Removing barnacles from your skin begins to remove the barnacles from your brain, which will allow positive thoughts to enter your mind and body.

Without healing there is no health.

When making a decision, details matter.

Give yourself permission to be successful.

Give yourself an opportunity to have a transformation.

Wherever you are on life's journey, there is an opportunity for positive change.

Become a champion in your own league.

Sometimes one key can open many doors.

Be happy even when your expectations are not met.

Don't sweat the small stuff.

Believe you are good enough to take care of yourself.

Become free.

Your life's story, in the end, is how you have lived it. Make it sweet, happy, and healthy.

Learn from yourself.

Allow the unique you to blossom.

Develop your unique power.

Your life's story is based on you developing it.

You have the ability to develop your life story.

You have it in your power to....

Allow yourself to take a chance.

Eat your success.

Develop the world future yesterday.

Invent the future today.

Water-rich foods—the best diet plan.

Index of Sayings

Let others help you by taking the first step.

Free those you love.

Don't deal with what you could have done. Deal with what you are going to do.

Become a champion in your own division.

The right key can open many doors.

Become free to be yourself.

Just be.

Embrace the little things you do; they may really be big things.

Honor yourself.

Try laughter when you are in pain.

See sunshine in gray skies.

Many different problems have the same solution.

Your harshest critic may have become you yourself.

Let yourself speak.

Be prepared for your first success; it sometimes comes accidently.

Real truth is probably 70 percent of the real truth; 30 percent depends on individual interpretation. It is up to you to learn the real truth.

Understand the real truth of your life.

Learn who you really are.

Find your calling.

Learn from others but establish your own journey.

Champion your own decisions.

Be imperfect—get better skin and fewer blemishes.

Eat your medicine.

It's not the stress—it is how you respond to it.

Be careful with advice; it may come from a person's insecurities.

If you keep banging your head against the wall, you will have a headache no matter how many pain relievers you take.

Inhibitions increase with age, so stay young.

The least of us may become the best of us.

Unlimited possibilities.

Heal yourself; allow the unique you to blossom.

Handouts may turn into holdouts.

Handouts may reduce your potential.

Handouts don't always pay out.

Be comfortable with who you are not who you could have been or should have been.

Realistic expectations can go beyond what you are theoretically entitled.

You never know until you try.

Delete negative self-talk.

Positive self-talk encourages a positive outcome.

Youth Building—the path to positive self-talk.

Replace cultural stress and negative self-talk with a positive attitude.

Youth Building neutralizes cultural stress.

Reduce stress to increase total body hydration.

Eat your sunscreen.
You are never too old to create new opportunities.

Give yourself permission to be loved.

Allow your true passion to enter.

Give yourself permission to have a passion.

Creating a Healthy Life

Developing your passion is a major step along the journey to happiness.

Make an appointment with yourself.

Forgive yourself.

Handouts may not be helpful.

Focus on what you do, not what you do.

Allow your disability to transform your abilities.

Learn by watching without judging.

Don't let others embarrass you.

Don't judge others when they embarrass themselves.

Reconcile yourself to the truth, and then make the best of it.

Don't allow your disability to brand you.

Powerful lessons taught can have a powerful impact on the teacher as well as the student.

Learn from your mistakes.

Many of our life lessons emanate from mistakes we have made.

Real change only happens when you create your own.

You need to become yourself. Do what fits —what you eat, what you wear, how you spend your time—not what you think others expect of you.

Your skin is connected to your heart. Make your heart happy and your skin will become more beautiful.

You will be most happy when your loved ones are happy.

Be happy when you see happiness in others.

Eat to hydrate your brain, allowing happiness to enter.

Also by the Author

Dr. Murad is a world-renowned dermatologist, a qualified surgeon and trained pharmacist, in addition to authoring several successful books.

He has written five books, earning him a worldwide reputation as an authority on slowing down the ageing process.

His over-reaching philosophy is that truly healthy, beautiful skin can only be achieved by an inclusive, three pronged approach to health. Topical, internal and emotional self-care all combine in slowing down the ageing process and creating beautiful skin.

His other books include:

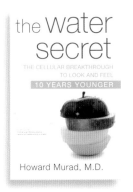

The Water Secret

Dr. Murad shares his scientifically proven strategy, "The Science of Cellular Water", and explains how damaged cells that leak water can lead to premature ageing. He shows that boosting cellular strength leads to a more youthful, more beautiful you.

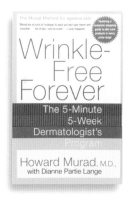

Wrinkle Free Forever

Dr. Murad has studied the effects of the environment on skin and ageing for thirty years, and the revolutionary methods he has developed to counteract those effects are packed into this book. The secrets which keep skin looking youthful are revealed, along with how to reverse damage that has already been done.

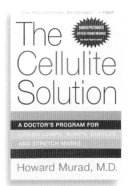

The Cellulite Solution

The first scientific roadmap to help reduce dimpling and improve stretchmarks! Dr. Murad outlines how simple nutritional modifications can provide the body with all the tools it needs to repair uneven, lumpy skin. Cellulite is a skin problem, not a weight problem.

www.murad.co.uk

Skincare for every skin type!

Whatever your skin priority there's a Murad range to transform your skin

Problem Skin

Blemish Control – Treat and prevent blemishes
Anti-Ageing Blemish Control – Combat blemishes and signs of ageing
Redness Therapy® – Calm and soothe sensitive/dry skin

Anti-Ageing

Age Reform® – Anti-ageing for all skin types
Environmental Shield® – Protection against premature ageing and sun damage
Resurgence® – Restoring youth's glow

Other Skin Priorities

Pore Reform® – Eliminate blackheads and minimise pores
Hybrids™ – Skincare meets makeup
White Brilliance™ – Brighten, illuminate and even skin tone
Murad Man – Strengthening men's skin defences
Age-Proof Suncare – Anti-ageing plus sun protection
Bodycare – Reducing cellulite and stretchmarks